The Art of
Double Bass Playing

Warren A. Benfield

Professor of Music, Northwestern University
and De Paul University, and member of the
Chicago Symphony Orchestra. Formerly with
the Minneapolis Symphony, St. Louis
Symphony, and Philadelphia Orchestra.

James Seay Dean, Jr.

Associate Professor of English, The University of Wisconsin-Parkside. Formerly Assistant Professor of English and Music Associate,
Wright State University, Dayton, Ohio.

summy-birchard company
Evanston, Illinois 60204

Library of Congress Cataloging in Publication Data

Benfield, Warren.
    The art of double bass playing.

    1. Double bass—Instruction and study.
I. Dean, James Seay, 1938-   joint author.
II. Title.
MT320.B45   787'.41'0712   73-15788
ISBN 0-87487-081-X

Preface

This book sets out to complement the traditional bass methods by approaching the double bass from musical as well as technical standpoints. Based on years of teaching and orchestral experience, it is written for the student, teacher, and professional player. It considers the musical and technical aspects of performance, using the body and the right and left hands in playing, then takes up the double bass as an ensemble instrument in lessons, classes, orchestras, and auditions. Musical examples provide illustrations of how, through artistic means, the double bass can be seen for the musical instrument that it is.

We wish to thank those bass players and others who have been instrumental in making this book what it is. For what the book is not and for its imperfections, we are, of course, solely responsible. The photographs were taken by James Benfield. Encouragement and suggestions have come from many, especially Bertram Turetzky (the University of Southern California), David Walter (The Manhattan School of Music and the Juilliard School of Music), Henry Portnoy (principal bass, the Boston Symphony Orchestra), Roger Scott (principal bass, the Philadelphia Orchestra), and Joseph Guastefeste (principal bass, the Chicago Symphony Orchestra).

This book also owes much to the encouragement from our families, to the example of those colleagues and teachers from whom we have learned, and to the inspiration of those bassists, like Anton Torello and David Babcock, who have gone before us.

WAB and JSD

Contents

illustrations follow page 16

I.

The Double Bass: A Musical Instrument

When we read in Leopold Mozart's *Treatise on the Fundamental Principles of Violin Playing* (1756) that this musician had heard double basses performing "concertos, trios, solos . . . with great beauty," and when we hear of the achievements of Domenico Dragonetti and Giovanni Bottesini, and listen to the recorded performance of Serge Koussevitsky and the live concerts and recordings of Gary Karr and Bertram Turetzky, we know that the double bass can be a musical instrument if it is in the hands of a musical double bassist. Of course, the limitations of the instrument for solo playing should be recognized, both for the physical difficulty of playing soloistic passages musically, and for the economic difficulty of making a living as a double bass soloist in the meager repertoire. Lately, though, that repertoire has been increased, thanks to commissions from prominent players. Nevertheless, this instrument plays an important role in the present symphony orchestra. It provides the musical depth, the harmonic foundation, and the rhythmic power that give the orchestra its vitality.

The satisfaction of playing the double bass must lie, for the most part, in recognizing these factors and seeing the essential value of the bass as an ensemble instrument. To be a double bassist (excluding the jazz player for the moment) means playing in an orchestra. Orchestral playing, like solo playing, requires a high degree of musicianship and technique. The orchestral bassist must be able to sight-read well and to have a highly developed sense of ensemble playing. Accompanying artistically is difficult, for it requires an understanding not only of the individual part, but also of the entire score. Besides watching the conductor, the player must listen in order to fit with the ensemble. Chamber music playing, in developing this sensitivity, is excellent preparation for orchestral playing. For the double bass player this is particularly true, since the bassist gets satisfaction from conceiving his role in relation to the rest of the score. Only in this way can he understand just how his part fits in with the rest of the symphony. For example, the triplet motif at the beginning of Strauss' *Don Juan,* if begun with an accent will point up this passage so that it obviously belongs with similar passages in the other parts:

1

Sensitivity to the other parts is equally essential in the
Allegretto Scherzando from Beethoven's Eighth Symphony:

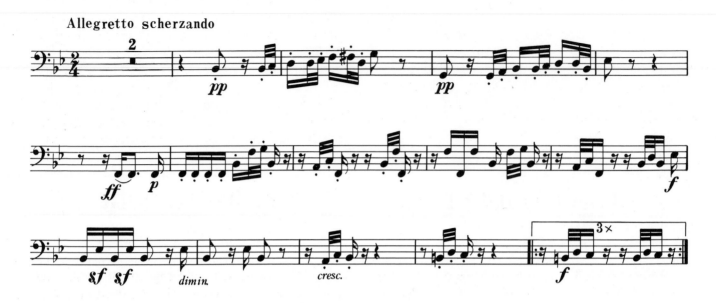

That understanding makes up for the few notes that punctuate the many rests, or the many difficult notes that are lost to the audience.

The bass player would do well to consider that at all levels of competence the most essential part of being a musician is the ability to understand the composer's meaning. Difficult passages may occur in exercises as well as orchestral operatic parts. The professional pulls out his pencil and marks the phrases and the beats. And if the professional is also a teacher, he will get his students to follow that practice. Too often the teacher forgets to tell his students all the little things he himself does. He is so engrossed in teaching the first etude, the second, the third that he forgets that the student must learn to make music out of the notes.

It is helpful to play from rented opera parts, for those parts, invariably marked, reveal the practical experience of others. Difficult passages make quick sense when marked with slashes through the beats, "eyeglasses" help spot the tricky retards, circles call attention to key changes, and bold pencilled lines mark cuts. And if the student doesn't know the meaning of certain words, in German, for instance, he should look them up in a good music dictionary rather than a German dictionary, since the primary meaning of the word or phrase may not always be the same as its specialized musical one. Rehearsal time costs a lot of money, and the quicker the orchestra members catch on to the conductor's wishes, the happier he and the manager will be.

Besides the matter of economics, there is the musical reason for marking parts. Fingerings, and "idiot marks" of all kinds leave nothing to chance —the interpretation is determined. Decide on a fingering, bowing, and phrasing, and follow it. Establishing the musical meaning is much like learning a dramatic role. The actor studies his part by looking for the basic rhythm, the climax, and the pauses where he will breathe. What piece of writing would make sense without some kind of punctuation? Similarly, musical punctuation goes beyond observing the rests; it requires understanding the music. Further, as the punctuation of a piece of writing goes from beginning to end, so musical punctuation must go in only one direction— forward. The musical current flows constantly toward the end of the composition. The musician should ride that current, both carried by it and maneuvering within it, as it moves toward that final cadence.

Once the player has set his markings in his mind, he no longer needs those signs, for the earlier analysis has done its work. The student who has not studied the structure of the music he is playing is a superficial musician. Once he begins playing and then makes a mistake, heaven help him. He is so used to hearing the music one way that if he gets off the track, his lack of understanding of the nature of the music will prevent his being able to get back on course. To this end the bassist who knows form, theory, and composition thoroughly has an advantage. He can understand better what the music is about. He will be able to enjoy the other parts of the symphony when he has little to do because he can see the entire concept, as the conductor does. The double bass *can* be a musical instrument if the double bassist approaches the music with artistic intelligence and integrity.

CHOOSING AN INSTRUMENT

Of the stringed instruments in the symphony orchestra, the double bass is possibly the easiest to play passably well and the most difficult to play to perfection. Though all the instruments of the string family have similar technical problems, the great size of the bass exaggerates these problems. For example, how the bass player sits or stands when playing probably affects him more than it does, say, the violinist. Or because of the long string length of the bass, the left hand position directly affects intonation; there is more room for error. Before examining the matter of artistry in playing the double bass, it is useful to take account of various mechanical factors that contribute to artistic playing.

When buying a bass, get the best one you can for the money. Deal with a shop or store whose people know basses, who make basses, who repair them, and who play them. Their advice will be invaluable. Unlike some items, new in musical instruments is not necessarily best. In fact, a stringed instrument is never at its best when brand new. A bass needs time to be "played in"; it needs to develop a "memory." Should the instrument come from another climate, as is the case with basses imported to the U.S. from Europe, the instrument has to adjust to its new surroundings. Frequently, in the first season the top cracks near the tailpiece and must be glued. One solution is to open the top of the bass when it arrives and let the instrument become acclimated for several weeks. After regluing the top, the bass will seldom crack.

If the bass is to resonate, it must have a relatively thin top. Put your finger in the F-holes of several basses and notice the variation in thickness of the top from instrument to instrument. Too much wood produces an unresponsive bass with a dull sound. But a bass with too thin a top cannot support the considerable force exerted by the strings. Generally, basses today are made with curved backs. Unlike the basses with flat backs, those with curved backs have strength and flexibility and are able to weather atmospheric changes. To be durable, a bass should have an ebony fingerboard. Those made with softer woods are susceptible to furrowing that results in buzzing strings. Another factor affecting the resonance of the bass is its endpin. Like the soundpost inside the body of the instrument, the endpin transmits vibrations from the bass to the stage. The most effective tip, therefore, is one that sticks into the stage. Those rubber tips, obtainable from surgical supply houses, are best used, not when playing, but when transporting the bass.

Basses seldom come to the dealer in optimum condition for playing. Certain adjustments must be made. The soundpost should be set to produce the tone you wish. The bridge, even if of good quality, will frequently need to have its feet sanded so that they fit the exact curvature of the top of the bass. Otherwise it will not transmit all of the vibrations to the top. The height of the bridge determines the height of the strings from the fingerboard. If the strings are too high, they are difficult to press down, and if too low, are apt to buzz. These adjustments, made by a reputable dealer (ask your local symphony musicians whom they patronize), should be made before the bass leaves the shop.

One important factor in the tone of a bass is the quality of strings used. A gut string gives a warm sound and is easy to play. But because of its sensitivity to the weather, its tension can vary considerably, and it dries out, requiring replacement several times a season. Steel strings, on the other hand, produce a harder tone and are more difficult to press down to the fingerboard but are more constant in their tone, and are relatively impervious to atmospheric changes. They too must be replaced, but generally not more than once a year. If the bass is healthy and the top strong, then it can probably take the additional strain exerted by steel strings. Otherwise, the tension can be relieved through raising the tailpiece by inserting a block under it. All in all, steel strings are now in most cases the better choice.

A good tone is further a function of the bow. The bow generates the sound by vibrating the string. That bow must be strong enough to maintain the force imposed upon it, yet it must be supple enough to transmit the nuances of rhythm, tone, and volume intended by the player. The bow must become an extension of the power and spirit of the bassist.

Two bows are presently in use: the French and the German, the latter also known in variant forms as the Butler, the Simandl, and other names. Whatever the name, the essential difference between the two forms is the manner in which force is imposed upon the bow by the hand. Both bows employ a natural hand position. The French bow operates like the bows of other stringed instruments, with the hand placed on top of the stick (figs. 9, 10, 11). Power comes as the hand applies weight distributed between the index and little fingers and at right angles to the stick. The thumb serves as the fulcrum and distributes the weight fore and aft. The weight exerted by the hand comes from the natural weight of the arm and shoulder.

The German bow is slightly longer, has a wide frog, and is played in approximately the old gamba style (fig. 12). The considerable force achieved with this bow is the natural result of holding it from underneath in such a way that the torque developed by the arm automatically keeps the bow "into" the string. The index finger again supplies the force, but it is supported by the second finger and thumb. With the German bow, the little finger serves to hold up the bow and to direct it so that it moves at right angles to the strings.

Both bows can be used effectively. The German bow, because it stays more naturally on the string, may prove easier for beginning students. Its additional length may be an advantage. Which bow to use should be left to the discretion of the student and his teacher.

The bow works on producing friction between the hair and the string. To aid the hair follicles in grabbing the string, the use of rosin on the hair increases the coefficient of friction. Bassists are always searching for the ideal rosin. A good one should cause friction without sticking. It should have staying power, perform consistently, and leave a minimal residue of powder on the strings, the bow, and the bass.

With these facts about the instrument in mind, let us turn to the principles underlying artistic playing.

II.

Playing the Double Bass

THE BODY

Body balance is vital to playing the bass effectively. If all the body's weight is on the right foot, there will be no weight to press the string down. But if the player stands or sits squarely with his weight evenly distributed, he can shift that weight as needed to the left or right hand. He should lean the side of the bass squarely against the abdomen so that the instrument can balance itself without the aid of the left hand. To play on the E string he needs to be able to shift the lower side of the bass forward, at the same time turning his body slightly to the right (figs. 1, 2, 3, 5). Body English is not just for pool halls but for concert halls too. And as in golf, if the stance is balanced, the power can focus on a central point. On the bass that focal point is where bow and string meet. Here is the point where all the energy and mass are brought to bear upon the note. Because the conjunction of bow and string is so important, the setting of the bow must be natural to the player, or, to put it another way, the height of the bass should be adjusted so that the bow can cross the strings naturally at an angle of ninety degrees, without an inefficient arcing as it moves from frog to tip (fig. 4).

If the body is balanced, there is sufficient weight for the left hand to press the string firmly to the fingerboard, thus allowing for a better tone. If the weight is all on the bow side, then the left hand has no power, and vice versa. The principle is true whether standing or sitting, whether playing the bass, cello, piano, oboe, or violin. By standing or sitting squarely, body weight can be shifted to where it is needed.

Not only can body weight be used to advantage in playing the double bass, but the weight of the bass itself can also be used. The bass is a huge instrument, and any help that gets the string under control should be used. The weight of the bass leaning into the fingers can allow the fingers to relax while pressing down the string. You cannot pitch a ball if you are tense and off balance. François Rabat, the French jazz player, was not far off when he called a record he once made "Bass Ball"—the analogy with the sport was not misplaced. The bassist must be like the boxer or tennis player, who stands prepared, on the balls of his feet, ready to shift his weight one way or the other. The body must be in a state of balance.

The bass player needs a highly developed sense of rhythm. Rhythm is not simply a matter of mechanically reproducing through the bass what is on the printed page. A classic example of the necessity for going beyond the notes occurs in the second movement of Tschaikowsky's Sixth Symphony:

The rhythm is not based on a group of five, but rather on groups of two and three, occasionally switching to three and two. When a passage involves more than four notes, break it up into its rhythmic components. To give life to a rhythmic passage you must feel the pulse throughout your body. Hindemith's Sonata for Double Bass provides an example of the need for a good rhythmic sense:

Molto adagio (♪ 50-52)

By permission of B. Schott's Söhne Musikverlag, Frankfurt/M

Of course a bass player should not express the rhythm bodily, in some sort of grotesque ballet. A bassist's job is to provide sound. Leave it to the conductor to provide a visual manifestation of the beat. Clap out passages to isolate the rhythmic factor, subdividing them into, say, groups of two and three. In this way the total pattern becomes intelligible. You must be able to see both the forest and the trees, so to speak.

Rhythms are only approximated by the printed page. The notation itself can sometimes be a hindrance. Those dotted eighths and sixteenths are a case in point. The purpose of the sixteenth is to go to the next resting note, the dotted eighth. The real pattern is from short to long, though the way the figure looks on the page, it appears to go from long to short. By fingering the sixteenth to the resting note, the rhythm improves, as does the intonation. In general, remember that moving notes go to resting notes.

Breathing and Singing

The physical act of breathing is another aspect of string playing that should be given attention. If the bassist consciously matches his breathing to his musical phrasing, he can mold and punctuate the musical line better. Sing along with the part as you practice. Mark where you take a breath. Think of music-making as something physical, as the singer must. This helps to develop a cantabile sound.

Often what is essential to good singing is equally essential to good bass playing. We can learn much from studying with a good singer, especially in the matters of breathing and phrasing. The music can be made much more exciting if it is thought of in terms where breath lines become operative, as in the contemporary poetry of Lawrence Ferlinghetti and Allen Ginsberg where each unit is read in one breath. Engage your total self in the music. For example, in Beethoven's Eighth Symphony there is a tune in the third movement that can come alive when you comprehend it totally, actually breathing with its phrases:

Tempo di Menuetto

Another example is the Andante from Beethoven's Fifth Symphony, where proper breathing is needed to achieve the long musical line:

The student, to come back to our earlier thought, must do more than learn music with his eyes. He needs to learn to hear, feel, and play it over and over, because in this way he hears the music through the gut rather than through the brain. In fact, the study of solfege is considered so important by many European teachers that the student does not pick up the instrument to play an etude until he has learned to sing the music with syllables. So often conductors and teachers in Europe will say that if you can't sing it, you can't play it. The jazz people tell us the same thing.

Sing your exercises with syllables, preferably with the fixed *do* system (*do* is always C) so that you learn to hear the intervals. Singing the syllables as you learn the exercises allows your fingers to go automatically to the right spot. Some have taken their singing outside the practice room. Slam Stewart, the great jazz bassist, made his name by singing along with his bass. Though as symphonic bassists we generally do not have Slam Stewart's type of music to play, we can still experiment by singing along with our parts.

One of the most difficult things to learn is the ability to listen—really listen—to how you sound. Try tape-recording your practice sessions. This may provide you with a few surprises. You never knew you sounded so good (or bad), did you?

Scales and Arpeggios

Music is made from scales, intervals, and broken chords. You can't get away from the necessity of practicing them. Mastering them takes hard work, and there are no short cuts. But once learned, those scales and arpeggios will help you play better by making you immediately aware of the patterns in the music. The necessity of learning musical patterns can be compared to the necessity of learning phrases and complete thoughts in a foreign language. While pronunciation and accent of individual words may be perfect, you will never sound like a native unless you learn the intonation and "song" of the language as revealed in entire sentences. Do the same with scales. Look at the structure of the line you are playing and see whether it conforms to a scale pattern, or includes accidentals. The jazz man makes a quick analytical glance his usual practice. His part is most often written out with chord patterns, if he has any written part at all. The rhythm and chordal structure and sequence are all that are given.

Consider this example by Steve Rodby:

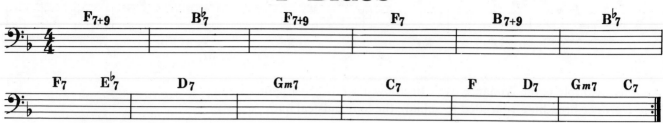

That brief indication of the chord changes is a far cry from the music that is actually made. Here is one way the piece can be realized:

Straight 8th notes are played ♪♪ ♪♪ as ♩ ♪♪ ♩ ♪

With so much being done for the bass today, the bassist owes it to his instrument to learn the contemporary repertoire. Improvisation is not just for jazzmen. The symphonic player when playing such music should apply to it the same standards and finesse that he gives to turning a Mozart cadence. Any verbal sounds should be correlated with the sounds from the bass. Here too rhythms should be exciting. The bassist should engage his whole body when playing so that he and the bass become one. Contemporary music is insisting on this identity, and bass players should make the most of it.

Besides singing, the bassist may be called on in much contemporary music to engage his "self" in other ways: clapping, snapping, whistling, and so forth. The notation looks wild, and the composer often cultivates his own symbols. New notation is needed to keep up with innovations of composers. Eventually, out of our notational chaos will come some universally accepted symbols. Bertram Turetzky has been in the vanguard in demonstrating and writing about the wide range of possibilities the bass offers the composer. Some one hundred and fifty works commissioned by him are witness to his success. To play much contemporary music it is not enough to have studied the Kreutzer etudes; special etudes must be devised that will help in playing that music. The composer must provide instructions for his piece in order to make sense from a score employing notational symbols not often introduced in bass methods. For his "Valentine" for solo contrabass Jacob Druckman, as an example, not only gives special instructions within the score, but he prefaces this rather short piece with two pages of explanation:

Since this score is written in analog notation the traditional rhythmic connotations of black and white notes are no longer valid. Black and white notes are used, instead, to indicate different methods of producing sounds. Approximate elapsed time is indicated above each line at five-second intervals. The actual space given to each five-second interval is larger on the first two pages than on the rest of the score to allow room for the extremely fast figures. In addition to the traditional arco and pizz., this work employs vocal sounds and sounds made with a soft, felt headed timpani stick. The placement of the various elements on the score is as follows:

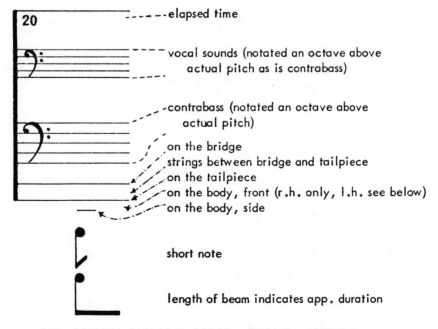

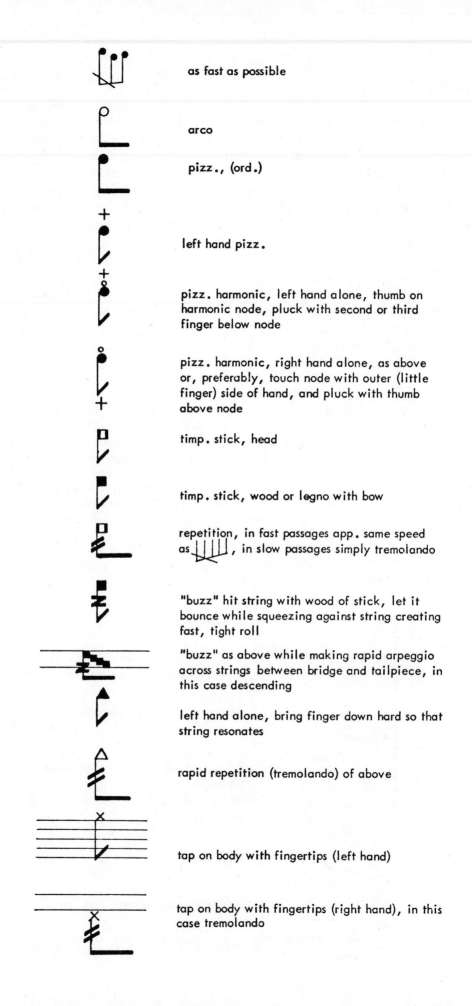

as fast as possible

arco

pizz., (ord.)

left hand pizz.

pizz. harmonic, left hand alone, thumb on harmonic node, pluck with second or third finger below node

pizz. harmonic, right hand alone, as above or, preferably, touch node with outer (little finger) side of hand, and pluck with thumb above node

timp. stick, head

timp. stick, wood or legno with bow

repetition, in fast passages app. same speed as ⊔⊔⊔⊔ , in slow passages simply tremolando

"buzz" hit string with wood of stick, let it bounce while squeezing against string creating fast, tight roll

"buzz" as above while making rapid arpeggio across strings between bridge and tailpiece, in this case descending

left hand alone, bring finger down hard so that string resonates

rapid repetition (tremolando) of above

tap on body with fingertips (left hand)

tap on body with fingertips (right hand), in this case tremolando

 indicates that tapping on body (fingertips or timp. stick) should change position so that timbre changes

 choke resonance of string by touching lightly with l.h. as in harmonics but not at a node

 pizz. notes of indeterminate pitch because of choking of string

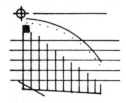 ricochet legno, left hand lightly stops strings to prevent distinct pitch of open strings; pitch heard is result of distance between bow and bridge (in this case bow bounces from pont. to tasto causing descending figure)

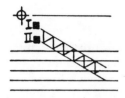 insert handle of timp stick between the indicated strings, beat rapidly from side to side while moving from pont. to tasto (in this case ⊕ indicates that strings are lightly choked; also appears without ⊕ indicating that pitch of open strings is added to the sound.

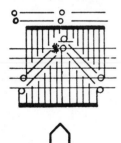 gliss. (arco) on I and II, touch lightly so that harmonics sound when fingers pass nodes, keep the fingers not at an exact perfect fourth so that harmonics will occur at different moments on the two strings

∧ traditional sul ponticello (arco on string near bridge)

Vocal sounds:

Phonetics are written in the International Phonetic Alphabet:

i	beet	bit		u	do	du
I	bit	bɪt		ə	among	əmʌŋ
ɛ	bet	bɛt		ʒ	measure	mɛʒəˑ
a	bat	bat		ʔ	glottal stop	
ɑ	dot	dɑt		~	nasal sound	
u	foot	fut				

 voiced (definite pitch)

unvoiced (whispered)

 inhaling (semi-voiced)

 voiced, indeterminate pitch (half spoken)

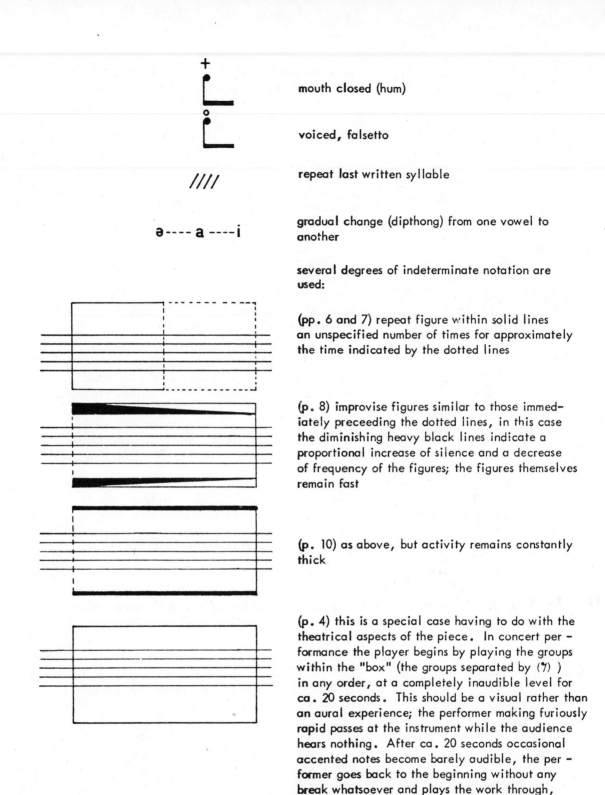

mouth closed (hum)

voiced, falsetto

repeat last written syllable

gradual change (dipthong) from one vowel to another

several degrees of indeterminate notation are used:

(pp. 6 and 7) repeat figure within solid lines an unspecified number of times for approximately the time indicated by the dotted lines

(p. 8) improvise figures similar to those immediately preceeding the dotted lines, in this case the diminishing heavy black lines indicate a proportional increase of silence and a decrease of frequency of the figures; the figures themselves remain fast

(p. 10) as above, but activity remains constantly thick

(p. 4) this is a special case having to do with the theatrical aspects of the piece. In concert performance the player begins by playing the groups within the "box" (the groups separated by (⅂)) in any order, at a completely inaudible level for ca. 20 seconds. This should be a visual rather than an aural experience; the performer making furiously rapid passes at the instrument while the audience hears nothing. After ca. 20 seconds occasional accented notes become barely audible, the performer goes back to the beginning without any break whatsoever and plays the work through, ignoring the "box" and playing the figures in the order written. (This is why the time indications begin at 20 seconds.)

In sum, it is important to employ your total body when playing. You must grasp the basic part of the particular music you are playing—its rhythm—so that it becomes a part of you. For that to happen, your body must be a balanced instrument, sensitive to musical needs. Then you should understand the musical line and its harmonic nature, and be able to sing the part. Finally, it is very important to develop the ability to hear yourself. When you learn to hear yourself, you are able to criticize and hence improve your playing.

THE RIGHT HAND

Tone and the Bow

Perhaps the most important, yet often the most neglected, aspect of bass playing is that of producing a good tone. Of course the bass should be played rhythmically and in tune, but it is beyond rhythm and intonation that music lies. Tone, with its necessary accompanying factor, insight into the composer's idea, makes for musical playing. A good tone marks a good player.

The most important point in producing a tone is to concentrate on drawing the sound with the bow. Sound emanates, not from where the fingers of the left hand stop the string, but from the point where the bow and the string meet. Though most bass methods, notably those of the German school, do a good job of teaching the positions, develop-

ing good tone often depends on the luck of finding a good teacher.

What, then, is tone, and how is it made? The string spins in sine waves, so the physicists tell us (figs. 24, 25). The weight of the bow must not cut off that spin. The bow's weight plus speed equals the sound. That, with the bow's position on the string, will determine the tone. Often students who play very well otherwise, bow too close to the fingerboard. The simple action of moving the bow closer to the bridge will produce a further series of overtones, thus yielding a bigger and more powerful sound. This is really where tone is made.

Experiment to find the *best* tone, which may not necessarily be close to the bridge. For example, in Verdi's opera *Otello*, the bass solo at the beginning of Act IV begins on an accented low E:

From experimenting you find that the bass speaks best, not where you would generally expect it to, closer to the bridge, but rather over the fingerboard, with the E natural begun with the bow on the string. An inch lower with the same weight and the bass only squawks. From that lowest note the same tonal quality must be kept in rising to the upper register. It is necessary to experiment for the best tone to play wide-ranging solo passages. In contrast to the right hand, the left hand is strictly doing tricks, though of course the ear has to be developed so that the fingers are put in the

right spot on the fingerboard. But it is the right hand that is the secret of good tone.

When learning the positions on the bass, it is important also to remember as you go up on the scale to move the bow closer to the bridge (fig. 6). The security of staying closer to the fingerboard is only apparent, and the contraction of the right and left hands is frequently a sign of fright. Consider the motif in Strauss' *Ein Heldenleben,* where you must play close to the bridge to have the power and breath to get through the phrase, particularly if the conductor takes it slowly:

Lebhaft bewegt

A few months of experimenting, most often by playing closer to the bridge, will make a great difference. Students think the teacher has worked wonders and speak about how he has improved their sound, when all he did was to move their bow an inch or so down on the string.

It is most important for the string player to pay attention to how the bow moves on the string; there should be a follow-through, as in swinging a golf club or tennis racket. What happens after the contact with the string is very important. Instead of just pulling and pushing the bow, the bass player should draw the bow—an action that carries on beyond the time the bow plays the note. Although he may not have played golf or tennis, for some reason he often knows something about pool. Most players (pool and bass alike) will understand at once the comparison of drawing that cue stick to drawing the bow. As in pool, too much downward action produces a scratch. The bow is to be drawn without pressure. Words like pressure or force give the wrong impression. The weight of the arm should be used so the sound will not be killed. Pressing into the string destroys that rotation of the string about its various harmonic nodes. The bow's weight and speed must be in phase or in sympathy with the motion of the string.

The action of the bow is to draw the string much the way a steam shovel scoops the earth. The bow's hair follicles must be moving past the string in sympathy with the string's spin. The bow must fit the action of the string, not the other way around. This is what drawing the bow means. The fit between bow and string must be like the fit when the cogs of gears mesh. Pushing and pulling the bow are like stripping the gears. To produce a good tone the bow and string must agree: a good draw, a good tone (figs. 7, 8).

Another analogy may help give the idea of this action. The bow is like a hand saw; both can bind if too much pressure is applied. Where most of us when sawing get the bite only on the down strokes, and not at all evenly, a professional carpenter gets the bite going both ways. He makes the saw work for him by drawing it evenly through the wood so that it doesn't bind. Consequently he can get through the wood in six strokes where it takes us twelve, and he does so with a more even cut—we almost said sound or tone. The old joke about the bass player sawing away in the orchestra may not be far off the mark. Now, once the bow has been drawn past the string, the follow-through as it leaves the string becomes important. This can be likened to throwing a ball. Some people throw with their wrists, others with their arms, and some, the good ones, follow through. In bass playing the follow-through motion produces that drawing motion, as the bow becomes an extension of the arm.

Tone is a matter of getting the string to vibrate fully on every note. The result we are after is a good sound. LeRoi Jones put it this way: "HOW YOU SOUND?? is what we recent fellows are up to." What's good for his poetry is here good for music. Listen to yourself. When you can really hear yourself, you improve. Yet this problem of listening to your tone is one of the hardest things to learn.

At times a passage may only seem to be posing difficulties for the left hand. For instance, one student had a problem playing a chromatic scale for one octave on the D string in one slurred bow. As his left hand moved faster, his right hand started spinning out—the bow started going too fast, following the left hand. The trick is to make the hands work independently of each other, to be able to pat your head and rub your stomach, so to speak. In isolating the problem, it becomes apparent that the trouble is not with the left hand getting all the notes, though indeed they may not all be there, but with the right hand providing enough power to get through the scale. The student was asked to play on one note for three full counts, then six, then for thirteen. After getting enough length from the bow for the scale, then getting the notes was relatively simple. As an example, consider the slurred chromatic scale from that favorite audition piece, the Overture to Wagner's opera *Der Fliegende Holländer*:

Allegro con brio

In passages such as this one it is especially important that the hands work independently. The right hand must not know what the left is doing. By working out the passages with each hand separately, this part, like most, can be learned more quickly. First develop enough bow for the scale, then finger that scale with just the left hand. Afterwards put both hands together. Practicing each hand separately is something that is seldom done by bass players anymore, though pianists haven't given up this technique. What's good for the pianist is also good for the bassist.

It also helps to watch the bow when playing. See if it is going too fast or too slow. The bow's speed should be measured and should match the vibration of the string. A poor *détaché* stroke is usually caused when the bow is out of phase with the string (and is what makes Mozart difficult to play well). A common fault in playing chromatic passages like the one above is to muddle the last few notes in preparing to get the last note. Once you recognize that the bow, and not so much the fingers of the left hand, is usually at fault, you can concentrate on correcting the bow. First the bow, then the fingers. These are technical matters, but the mastery of such problems has a musical purpose, whether you are a beginner or a professional. The notes of a fast passage, if they were magnified, should have as much beauty as those in a slow cantabile passage, such as the opening of Bach's Aria from the Suite No. 3:

A fine tone, then, is a *sine qua non*. And the bow is primarily responsible for generating tone.

Sometimes the beginning student is asked to play a scale in triplets: *do do do, re re re, mi mi mi*, etc., or perhaps with four bows per note: *do do do do, re re re re*. This seemingly meaningless exercise allows him to look at the bow to see that the string is vibrating correctly and that the bow is being drawn rather than being pushed or pulled. He should be sure to place the bow on the string before playing. For example, take part of one of Isaia Billè's exercises (*Nuovo Metodo*, No. 263, p. 22):

If he doesn't set the bow into the string before beginning the second down-bowed note, he can easily lose rhythmic control. The bow should be planted. Otherwise it begins to get a mind of its own, and hacks away out of control. Many students, when they play a difficult passage, become excited and begin to play vertically; the bow comes down on the string instead of moving horizontally. Horizontal playing can be misunderstood too. Sometimes it can be too long. A series of notes ♩ ♩ ♩ ♩ ♩ ♩ can be played, lengthening their duration, with any portion of the bow from tip to frog, and with any length of that bow. Whether the notes are played almost entirely on the string as, say, in Wagner's operas, or shorter, as in Mozart's symphonies, they must always be played horizontally rather than vertically by the bow. If as a regular practice the string is hit from above (as in some Bartók and Stravinsky), control of the bow can be lost. Try playing both vertically and horizontally in the opening of the Finale to Tschaikowsky's Fourth Symphony to see the difference:

15

It is important to learn to be flexible, to be able to play notes as long or as short as you desire. When it comes time to find out about the characteristics of an orchestra for which you plan to audition, you want to know whether it is an orchestra that favors "long" or "short" playing. The Philadelphia generally favors long; the Boston and Cleveland, short; and the Chicago, fifty-fifty, depending on the conductor. Short or long, the bow can only really be controlled when it meets the string horizontally.

By experimenting with extremes of interpretation you are better able to give the conductor what he wants. If he should call for a *flautando*, you need the control that only horizontal playing, playing on the string, can give. As we noted, in playing the *Otello* passage with its low accented E, you find by experimenting that the string speaks best when the bow plays over the fingerboard. As a general rule, when playing arco on the two lower strings, play fuller and nearer the fingerboard and, on the two upper strings, play nearer the bridge to produce the most musical and centered tone. The trick is to get such a focussed tone, and only the ear can judge best where or how you get it.

Pizzicato

The art of playing pizzicato, so highly developed by jazz players, has until the advent of the new breed of bassist been traditionally neglected by the symphonic player. Yet the art of playing pizzicato is no less important than playing arco. Both involve the right hand, both produce in the last result the sound the bass makes. One teacher has said to think of the bass as a harp. Lead the string rather than work it like a slingshot. Fritz Reiner's famous directive was: "Don't give me slingshot pizzicato." With care, pizzicato can be made an artistic sound. Producing pizzicato is much like producing a bowed sound: both require attention to attack and release. The sound can be a short staccato plunk or a ringing arco sound made with the left hand kept down firmly. Meanwhile the violins, who pay little attention to pizzicato, go "pop, pop, pop." Of course, the bass has the advantage of its long string length. Frequently students will play pizzicato without thought as to its production: one goes sideways, one goes up, another plays with his thumb.

There are many ways to play pizzicato, but it must be done artistically. Earlier we said that you should move closer to the bridge as you ascend the scale in playing arco. In pizzicato as you ascend the scale, you should do the opposite and play closer to the left hand. In fact, when playing the pizzicato harmonics in Ravel's *Ma Mère l'Oye* it is more effective to play the pizzicato above, not below, the left hand, afterwards letting go with the left hand immediately, the way a harpist does in using his palm to sound the harmonic. Harpists do this, although they use only the middle of the string, because they have so many strings that it is not necessary to use any of the other harmonics on one given string. They use the base of the palm of the hand and pluck with the same hand, which automatically makes them leave the string after plucking the string. The bassist will find that by borrowing this technique from the harpist, harmonic pizzicati will ring clearer in the Ravel passage and also in Debussy's *Jeux*, where the same situation arises.

By playing closer to the bridge on the lower strings and closer to the left hand on the upper strings the right hand can follow an arc upward as the scale ascends (figs. 19, 20, 21). Pizzicato arpeggios come off more naturally this way, following the path of the arm. If such passages were played straight across, the motion would become impeded. Nevertheless, it is important to experiment to find the place and angle that produce the desired sound.

It is sometimes useful to use more than one finger to play pizzicato passages. In the Scherzo from Tschaikowsky's Fourth Symphony it helps to play the ostinato section by alternating the first and second fingers:

Fig. 1. Standing, with French bow (front view)

Fig. 2. Standing, with French bow (side view)

Fig. 3. Standing, with French bow (rear view)

Fig. 4. Sitting, with French bow

Fig. 5. Standing, with German bow

Fig. 6. Standing, with French bow, thumb position

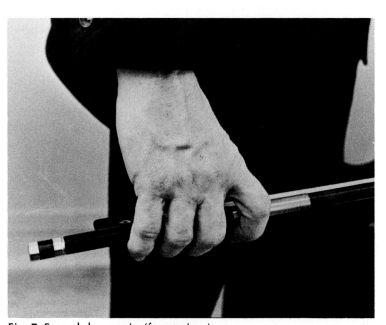

Fig. 7. French bow grip (front view)

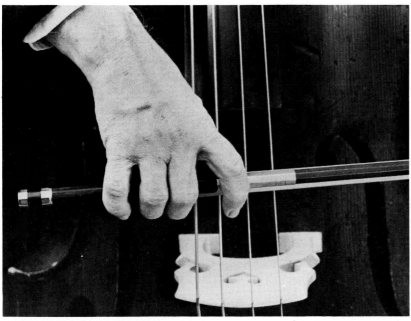

Fig. 8. French bow grip (front view)

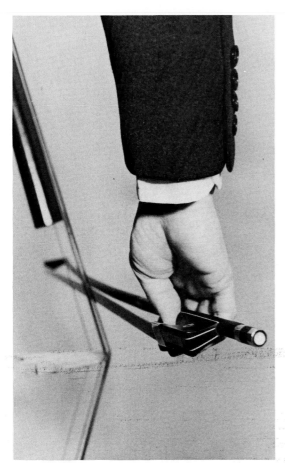

Fig. 9. French bow grip (side view)

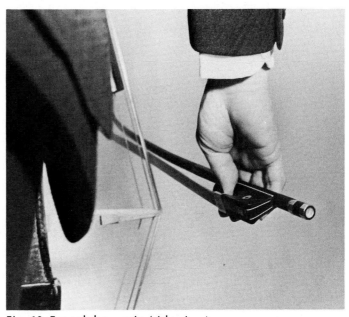

Fig. 10. French bow grip (side view)

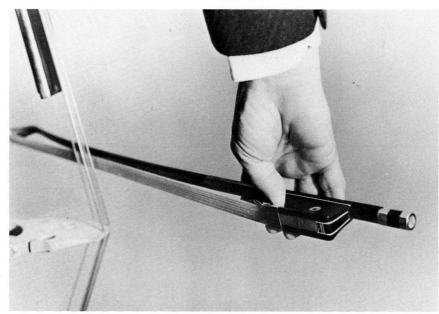

Fig. 11. French bow grip (side view)

Fig. 12. German bow grip

Fig. 13. Left hand in lower position

Fig. 14. Left hand moving through thumb positions

Fig. 15. Left hand moving through thumb positions

Fig. 16. Left hand moving through thumb positions

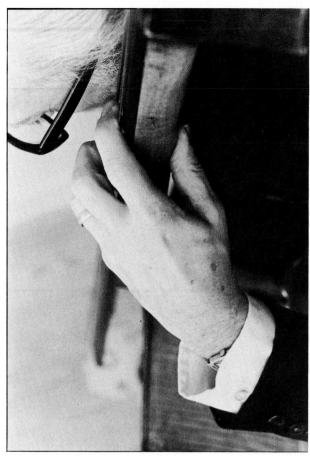

Fig. 17. Left hand (side view)

Fig. 18. Left hand (side view)

Fig. 19. Pizzicato with two fingers

Fig. 20. Pizzicato with thumb

Fig. 21. Pizzicato with second finger

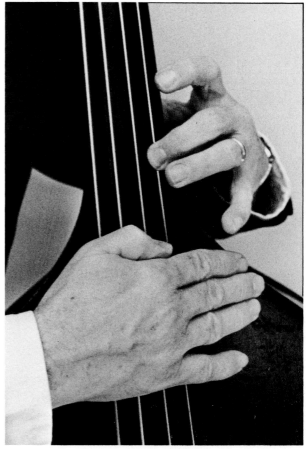

Fig. 22. Vibrato, developing rhythm

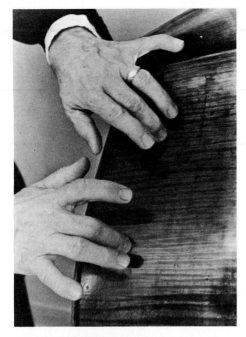

Fig. 23. Vibrato, developing proper motion

Fig. 24. Harmonic nodes on vibrating string

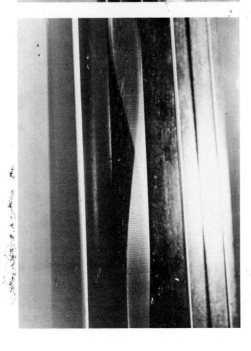

Fig. 25. Harmonic nodes on vibrating string

Another passage played pizzicato, but at a slow tempo, is the slow movement from Sibelius' Second Symphony, where the basses have:

The art of playing pizzicato can be carried to a high degree, as recent virtuosi have demonstrated. Symphonic players can learn a great deal from jazz bassists, who more than any other group have achieved success with pizzicato sounds. The student should be advised to give great importance to the production of pizzicato sounds. The biggest mistake the beginning student can make is that he does not stop the string solidly enough with his left hand. The result is a "punk" sound. If the string is pressed solidly, then there is a rich sound. Incidentally, pizzicato is an excellent way to strengthen the left hand and to learn to control it. And the student shouldn't wait until he is halfway through the method book to take up pizzicato. He should learn it right from the start. As he practices etudes it is often good for him to lay the bow down, and, while learning the left hand, learn to play pizzicato.

The variety of techniques that apply to arco playing also apply when playing pizzicato. Like the bow, the right hand playing pizzicato can move up and down the strings for different effects, though the traditional orchestral repertoire usually calls for the normal "long" sound made with either the first or second finger. Composers today call for more extensive and varied pizzicato, ranging from the short defined variety produced by the fingernail to the sustained lyric tones made by using the thumb in guitar fashion. Additionally, contemporary composers may require double and triple stops, slurs, glissandos, tremolos, harmonics, including raised harmonics made by pulling the string to the side, as in guitar and sitar playing, and, for the left hand, pizzicato created by percussive fingering. Some of these techniques are considered in Lunsford Morris Corzine's edition of Findeisen's *Complete Method for String Bass*, and in Bertram Turetzky's publications, such as his "Notes on the Double Bass" (*The Bass Sound Post*, Vol. 7, No. 5 [1968-69], pp. 9-16).

When playing pizzicato, the action of the left hand becomes critical to the tone and articulation in a greater degree than when playing arco. Pizzicato, especially in legato passages, calls for a firm left hand, since the string's vibration, caused as it is by a percussive attack, is harder to control. Once mastered, though, the left hand technique can complement that of the right by producing a range of variations in tone, vibrato, and articulation.

Especially today, the symphonic bassist should become adept at many forms of pizzicato. Composers have discovered the great potential of the instrument for producing a wide range of plucked sounds, thanks to the influence of jazz musicians. Where once pizzicato meant simply a non-bowed note to the orchestra musician, now the distinction between jazz and classical technique cannot be made so neatly. Many of the younger bassists, frequently doubling as jazz musicians, are paying more attention to producing a variety of pizzicato sounds. Conversely, for the jazz bassist the bow is becoming a regular part of his equipment. The integration of both techniques into both areas cannot but help to raise the standard of playing to a level closer to the potential of the instrument.

THE LEFT HAND

Both the right and left hands have a dynamic function in producing music. Although the right hand is the one which generates the sound through the bow on the string, the left hand has more to do than simply stopping the string at appropriate lengths. For this reason the matters of shifting and positions will be taken together, followed by a few words on vibrato. First, though, consider how a string player learns.

Tactile Memory

A musician's memory is generally tactile. If he can memorize certain patterns in his muscles, he can free himself from reading separate notes and can think more about the musical line of the composition at hand. Difficult passages can be simplified by recognizing sequences of patterns. Take the first important bass passage in Weber's *Euryanthe* Overture. The left hand begins on A and fingers: 1 4 1 4 1 4—0 1 1 4 2 4. Note that the second half of the measure repeats the first pattern, though the sequence begins on G. Here are the two sequences as they alternate:

The first thing is to get the right hand to do the triplet bowing  until every note sounds the same, down- or up-bow. In a group of three notes (or four) the second note and not the first is the most important one. This is where the tempo is set. It's like cutting a piece of pie. The second cut determines the size of the slice. (But then one thinking student demolished that theory. "What," he asked, "if you cut the pie in half?")

Next, to the left hand. Practice the first two notes:

in tempo: that is important, because then not only is the right hand working in tempo, but the left hand will also be in tempo with it. Then play three notes, making the shift, and repeat:

Then add the fourth note:

and so forth to complete the first pattern.

Learn the second pattern in the same way: two notes, three, four, five, then six:

Each group starts out a note lower, alternating the first pattern with the second. It would also be beneficial here to learn the A flat major scale. Traditional music is made up of scales and broken chords. Pablo Casals begins every morning's practice with them. Look at a scale and take note of any accidentals. Recognize the scale pattern, and observe any variations from it. Efficient sight-reading depends upon this technique. Rather than looking at individual notes, look to what the passage means musically. The musical eye will see, not a blur of black notes but a chordal progression or a scale that constitutes an artistic line. Approached in this architectural way and not note by note, such difficulties as those in Elgar's Second Symphony or in most of Nielsen's symphonies will be more easily solved.

In the *Euryanthe* Overture, the second passage is also troublesome.
Learn the passage by memory, without constant reference to music.

By first playing two notes, B C, then three, B C A, then four, B C A E, in one motion of the left hand, and more until the whole pattern has been learned in terms of what finger goes where, then being aware of the position becomes of secondary concern. In the above passage the pattern B C A E is best played by throwing the hand back to the A, so that the first finger plays the A and E in one motion, bridging it the way guitar players do. Relax—let the fingers do the walking in such places. And if your shoulder begins to tense and hunch up, relax and drop it. The body as a whole must be in a natural position so that the hands can bring sufficient weight to bear on the string. To help learn the fingering of such passages, try first playing pizzicato, as suggested, then arco. Such practice helps avoid nervousness. The passage is learned on the basis of sound, not sight. Sound is,

after all, what we are after. By thinking too much about systems of fingering, the intellect, through the eyes, gets in the way of the hands as it tries to keep ahead of the notes. Musicality inevitably suffers, as does the unfortunate listener. But by the method outlined above, even the most difficult passages come more easily.

Both hands need to be trained to feel the patterns. Jazz bass players are often musical because of their highly developed tactile memory. Because their fingers are supple they retain the music in their fingers well, even though they frequently have difficulty reading with their eyes. By memorizing passages, jazz bassists are able to play things that would be well-nigh impossible if read through the eyes. Problems similar to those in the *Euryanthe* Overture occur in Mendelssohn's *Italian Symphony:*

The passage can be broken down into more manageable units that the fingers can comprehend. It makes several patterns and, as with most passages, has a key to its pattern. This one is on the A string: B C# D# E, 1 4 2 4. The only half step is the 2 4; the other part of the passage is fingered consistently: 1 4 1 4, etc. As a general rule, finger in the direction of the passage, and try to get

roughly the same proportion of notes on each of the three lower strings. Something is wrong if there are eight notes on one string, only one note on the next, and six notes on another.

A final example, from Strauss' *Don Juan*, illustrates this principle of discerning the underlying pattern and its variants:

The two six-note sequences are remarkably similar. By learning each one by rote, first two notes, then four, then all six, the pattern can be perceived: two notes on the A string, four on the D, and six on the G string. The tactile memory understands this. If the player discovers to his horror that the passage is in four sharps, with accidental E sharp to boot, he may well literally clutch.

Learning the aural and tactile patterns and their exceptions makes difficult music become easier. Music is frequently difficult to the eye, but rarely to the ear. Learn the music through the ear, and through the fingers. Of course the bow must also be made to work evenly. When learning a piece,

do not exceed the speed at which the bow can be controlled. If the bow is working well and moving in tempo, and if for some reason the left hand gives out, the bow will make the passage sound as though all the notes are there—sometimes. Such faking has been known to salvage a difficult audition.

Rhythm

A passage can also be learned in terms of rhythmic patterning. In Strauss' *Also sprach Zarathustra* the following difficult passage with complex fingerings and rhythms can be performed better learning the rhythm first, then the bowing, and finally the fingering:

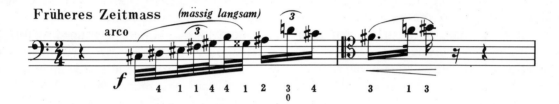

First sing the rhythm in slow four: duplet, triplet, duplet in one beat, then gradually go faster. Learn the fingering independently of the rhythmic pattern. In such passages, if you visualize the beats and mark where they fall, you will always arrive

on the beat. When sight-reading in an audition, this technique is essential. Consider these measures from Billè's *Metodo* (No. 263, p. 73); by locating the beats and landing precisely on them this apparently complex matter becomes simple:

The importance of rhythmic understanding is so vital that the third movement of Prokofiev's Quintet is written twice, in two rhythmic notations, so that the players can pick the version they comprehend best.

Breaking down passages in this way lessens the learning time. You may ask whether you can retain what you have mastered. Yes, it works! A student who learned very slowly because he "thought" too much and wouldn't relax enough in difficult passages was told of this type of learning as a way to teach beginning students. He said, "Why, that's what you had me do three years ago." And not having seen the *Euryanthe* Overture in several years, he was able to play it perfectly. The memory was still in his fingers. Often

we find that when listening to a familiar passage, the fingers begin to move in what the psychologist calls a conditioned response. That is musical memory.

Shifting and Positions

Shifting and positions are functions of each other, much like the parts of a slide rule. Two points should be made about shifting and positions. First, the positions should be learned across as well as up and down the fingerboard. The old-fashioned way of teaching positions by inching up the fingerboard generally ignores the lateral capacity and capability of a position. Secondly, the left hand should explore and become familiar with the limits of the string. To this end learn the lower and thumb positions concurrently. In this new way you avoid the awkward break in hand position and sound that frequently occurs between positions at the base of the neck. To alleviate this problem, smooth shifting is needed. Positions should be thought of simply as locations between shifts, points in a continuum of space and sound.

In learning positions across as well as up and down the fingerboard, think of how a slide rule operates. The slide must be able to go the limit of the stick, and its operation depends on reading across from one scale to another. By this mechanical process complicated arithmetical and logarithmic operations become simple, saving energy and time for more important tasks. Whatever the degree of difficulty, a few shifts of the slide and the answer is there. The left hand of the bass player acts much like that slide. That position he happens to be in doesn't really matter, and no

position should be more terrifying than any other. When the finger is on D on the G string, A, E, and B are across on the other strings.

The chart below shows that when the hand is in a particular position, certain notes are produced. The chart teaches the use of the first finger as a guide, not in a mechanical way (we have all seen chalk or pencil marks on necks of instruments), but in a musical way. This method also teaches intervals while teaching shifting. Too often the student squirms when he is asked to name or sing some such interval as a perfect 4th below C. By learning positions through shifting and by learning the other notes across the strings concurrently, he can learn to hear those intervals. He need not remember the name of the position he's in. That really doesn't matter as long as he can recognize the notes and can hear their sounds as played in that position. The name can come later.

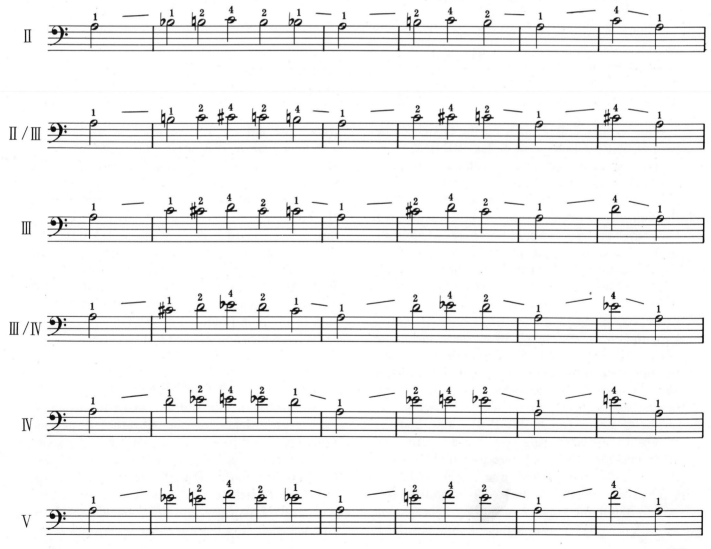

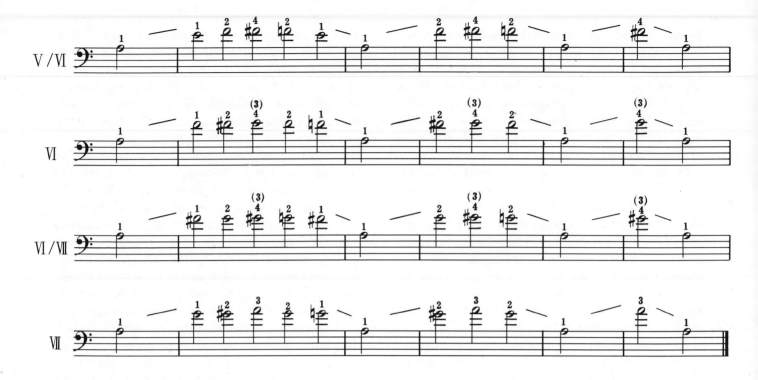

Execution: Using short tones and long tones with varying rhythms and bowing patterns.

Same bowing—smooth shifting.

With the first finger on A on the G string (the base or first position), find A flat or E flat. Now, on that A, learn the notes on all the strings in that position. Once you have committed those notes to the fingers, move from A to B flat. Shift rhythmically, and as with all shifts remember Bertram Turetzky's dictum: "There is no slow shift." Always shift fast, no matter what the tempo of the piece, no matter what the right hand is doing. Then as the first finger shifts from A to B flat, learn the notes under that position. Eventually you come to a shift from A to D, where your thumb, at the neck's base, finds anchorage more secure than that of the thumb in the first position. Some basses have E, and some, E-flat necks; you must find out which yours has. Think of the bass as having three basic reference points on the G string: the A, the E or E-flat, and the B. From these anchorings you can determine the other positions. Now you are prepared to go to the next half-step shift, and on to G sharp and A.

The bass student can quickly learn shifting this way, without the trauma of getting agoraphobia as he goes higher and higher in the positions.

Under the old method he often is so confused with memorizing just what fingers go where in what position that he becomes discouraged with his progress, or lack of it. "I'm only between second and third positions," he says, "with a total of seven—I'll never make it." By learning the entire fingerboard early, the student knows just what the limits of the instrument are and is not in the least frightened of the thumb positions. The purpose here is to be able to take the mind off the left hand so that more attention can be paid to the tone produced by the bow. The action of the left hand should become automatic.

Thumb Positions

To gain fluidity in shifting, learn the lower to the upper reaches of the fingerboard as one achievement. When you learn the half position, you can play the open strings G, D, A, E, and with the first finger, D-sharp, G-sharp, A-sharp, and E-sharp across. What is true there is also true exactly halfway up that string, where an octave higher, the harmonic G, D, A, and E are found. With the thumb on those harmonics, the first finger plays G-sharp, D-sharp, A-sharp, and E-sharp. The only difference, and that only if it suits you better, is to finger 1 2 3 rather than 1 2 4. This correspondence between the half position and the start of the thumb position, once recognized, should take the terror out of the heights of fingering. The thumb positions can become simply a matter of physical rather than mental agony.

By learning the thumb positions as you learn the lower positions you take away the bugbear attached to those upper positions. Frequently students who are competent at the lower positions sound like beginners in the thumb positions because they are not used to them. They consider these a separate aspect of bass-playing, tacked on to accommodate the quirks of composers like Strauss, Debussy, and Ravel, who surely must be out to embarrass the player. One benefit of learning the upper and lower registers together is the ensuing improvement in tone.

Now, you ask, how do you get your hand out of the regular positions and into the thumb positions? A cellist suggests that the thumb should be placed at right angles to the string, starting at about D on the G string (the fourth position), and then the hand should slide lightly up and down the fingerboard (figs. 14, 15, 16). The fingers will fall into their proper position naturally. The proper grasp for the left hand (and for that matter, the right too) is similar to the way a monkey grabs onto a branch and swings (figs. 13, 17, 18). When the music starts swinging, be sure to keep the fingers close to the fingerboard. You won't play any louder by hammering each finger down. Such fly-catching is wasted motion. Be sure, however, to press the string down firmly. And when you are playing a descending passage, keep the hand in position with all the fingers down, so that the next note is just a matter of lifting a finger. Consider, for instance, how much less effort is required to play this passage from the first movement of Mozart's G Minor Symphony faster and more accurately when you observe this law of the conservation of energy:

Without putting the other fingers down and with the fingers curved, just slide the thumb rhythmically up and down the string, from bottom to top. The arm has to follow a smooth arc.

When the hand is relaxed, just stop, put the fingers down, and there's the perfect thumb position. The old German system where the player gets up to F sharp, then turns the hand, releases the thumb, turns the hand sideways, and shifts into overdrive is so unnatural that it often shows up awkwardly in performance. Singers have to learn to smooth over the break in the voice from one register to another. Bass players in their own way have to learn the same thing about their instrument. There is nothing mysterious about learning the thumb positions, nothing that can't be learned in rudimentary fashion in about fifteen minutes.

Learn the positions as a function of shifting, and see shifting as something natural, ranging from the bottom to the top of the fingerboard. Use the four bass methods, the German school of Simandl, the French of Nanny, the Italian of Billè, and the Hungarian of Montag for their excellent exercises. What these writers have designed for the half position can now be tried in the thumb position as well, an octave higher. Pick and choose the appropriate exercises from each of these methods, as each method has its strong points.

Exercises

Franz Simandl's *New Method for the Double Bass,* 2 vols., rev. Fred Zimmerman (New York: Carl Fischer, Inc.) has long been the mainstay of bass teachers. Its brevity requires perfection at each stage, but that brevity may also explain its success in teaching positions. Edouard Nanny's *Enseignement Complet de la Contrabasse à 4 et 5 cordes,* 2 vols. (Paris: Alphonse Leduc et Cie.) gives numerous exercises employing varieties of fingerings and scales that the firmly committed student should find useful. Isaia Billè's *Nuovo Metodo per Contrabbasso a 4 e 5 Corde,* 7 vols. (Milano: G. Ricordi & C.) is particularly complete, pays careful attention to the bow, uses the fingering 1 3 4 rather than 1 2 4, and provides rewarding exercises. Lajos Montag's *Contrabass Tutor,* 4 vols. (Budapest: Kultura) contains an approach similar to Simandl's, but with more breadth. The bassist should not stop here, however. There are many other methods, including some of the jazz

methods (Ray Brown's, for instance), from which the player can get good instruction.

Certain studies should also be mentioned: Otto Rühm's *Progressive Etuden für Kontrabass,* 5 vols., (Wien: Verlag Doblinger), Wilhelm Stürm's *110 Studies,* 2 vols., ed. Fred Zimmerman (New York: International Music Co.), the Kreutzer Etudes, ed., as *18 Studies,* by F. Simandl and F. Zimmerman (New York: International Music Co.), Isaia Billè's *18 Studies in All Keys for 4 or 5 Stringed Contrabass* (Milano: G. Ricordi & C.), and Franz Simandl's *Gradus ad Parnassum,* 2 vols., ed. Fred Zimmerman (New York: International Music Co.). Consult also Murray Grodner's *Comprehensive Catalogue of Available Literature for the Double Bass,* 2nd edn. (Bloomington, Ind.: Lemur Musical Research, 1964).

Experimental Fingerings

Experiment to find the best fingering. The late Anton Torello, principal bass under Stokowski and Ormandy and teacher at Curtis, once said that when he was a bass student in Barcelona (his whole family were bass players) he wasn't given anything to eat until he knew his lesson. Sometimes he got very hungry. What he would do to learn etudes was to develop his fingerings. He would work out as many ways as possible to play a passage and learn them all. Then he would put the music away for a day or two, and when he tried all the fingerings again, one was usually clearly better than the others. He might have tried 1 2 3 rather than 1 2 4. Given a choice of 2 4 or 1 2, he used 1 2 going up the scale and 4 2 coming back. He would try to avoid a whole step between 2 3 and 2 4, for instance, E flat to F. Here, he used 1 4 instead of 2 4.

Most professionals will tell you that fingering is critical in playing dotted eighths and sixteenths. Make your shifts in the imaginary rest between the dotted eighth and the sixteenth. Notice what happens to the fingering when the rhythm changes in this scale passage:

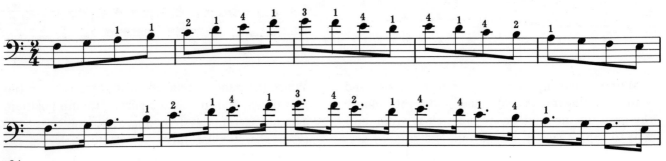

In going up the scale there is no difference in the fingering, but in coming back, the fingering should change, to take account of the rhythm. It is much easier to shift during that imaginary rest. The normal tendency is to play the sixteenths too soon. As Sir Georg Solti has said, in playing dotted eighths and sixteenths, you will never play the sixteenth too late, only too early. Shifting after the dotted eighth helps avoid that problem. Incidentally, the fingering in the first passage

above would work whether the passage was played fast or slow. The second fingering would not be good in a slow tempo, since here the dotted eighth needs to be sustained. Consider the dotted quarter and eighth rhythm in the first movement of Schubert's C Major Symphony. Though the dotted quarter and eighth are taken in one bow, that figure in sequence is best thought of as moving with the bow change from eighth to dotted quarter:

Extension Fingerings

Experiment then. Alternate fingerings are important. In auditions you may be asked to play a passage faster or slower than the way you have learned it. The fingering that works for one speed may not always work for another. But if you have prepared alternate fingerings and bowings, and— even more important—have experimented, you will be prepared for such changes. The fingerings sometimes imposed on the student by the teacher may not work for that student, for everyone's fingers are different: some short, some long, some thin, some thick. The bass player owes it to himself to find the fingering that suits him best.

Extensions are a personal matter and depend for their success upon the individual. Anton Torello said that you should just play the passage—it doesn't matter what finger you use. If you must use your thumb or your foot, then do so. There is an apocryphal story that in the Ginastera Concerto for Strings, Roger Scott, principal bass of the Philadelphia Orchestra, was seen using his nose to play a harmonic. It does, however, take some fantastic finger gymnastics to play the difficult passages.

It is helpful to learn to play scales in cello style, in one position. Take the E flat major scale:

Some bassists with very large hands are able to play a half step between fingers, but it takes daily practice to keep the hand stretched and the scales

in tune. In certain passages, as in the following from Mozart's E Flat Major Symphony, you can play more easily by employing extensions:

In short, shifting and positions are inextricably bound together and must be learned together. Shifting should be rhythmic, beginning with the base position (first finger on A on the G string). Accurate intonation of the intervals is necessary, as is an understanding of the theory of how the intervals relate—up and down and across the strings. Finally the parallel correspondence between the lower and upper positions for the thumb will become second nature if the entire fingerboard is learned as a unit. Experiment to find the most effective means to produce the most music.

Vibrato

Some say that it is impossible to teach vibrato. Others say that it is very difficult, and that a person has to be born with the ability to vibrate. It *can* be taught, and in a very short time. Since most people are right-handed, it is good to practice vibrato first with that hand, placing it on a table and vibrating the full arm with the necessary sideways motion (not a rolling or rocking motion, but rather a motion much like a trumpeter's hand vibrato). Then place the left hand next to the right on that table top, and get it to work in sympathy with the right. At first the left will tend to be somewhat spastic, but with a little practice, the two will work together in contrary motion (fig. 23). This motion can then be transferred naturally to the fingerboard.

There's a second way to achieve vibrato. While the student is playing, the teacher starts vibrating his hand the way it should go. Frequently this method works easily for the student. A third way is for the student to press his second finger down. The teacher puts his hand on the fingerboard below the student's hand. The student then rocks his hand back and forth in an arc and hits the teacher's hand with his little finger at about 140 to 160 vibrations per minute (fig. 22).

Now just as you vibrate in the lower positions, you should learn to do so in the upper positions. Perhaps you can do it well in the lower positions but are an utter failure in the upper half of the instrument. In the thumb positions, vibrato has to be sideways. Try playing an E with the second finger. Vibrate. Release the thumb. Feel the motion of the vibrato, then turn the hand and continue the vibrato with a sideways motion. Then move up, inching up an eighth of an inch at a time, vibrating all the way. Generally the higher you go, the faster the vibrato. Try to make its increase in frequency gradual so that there is no break from the lower positions to the thumb positions, just as the left hand should move smoothly and naturally into the thumb positions. At times, of course, the music may call for greater intensity, and hence you will want a faster vibrato, no matter where you happen to be on the instrument. An artistic use of vibrato can help color the music. The bass, more so than the other stringed instruments, is especially effective with its vibrato (as it is with its pizzicato) because of its wider range and longer string length. Gradually the bass player gets the feel of the motion required for vibrato. The trick is to avoid making a break as the hand turns sideways in going up the string. Find out what the hand does, what the full arm does. The motion should be involuntary, for if it is voluntary and measured, as some suggest, there is never a natural vibrato. There has to be an involuntary motion employing the full arm, with the elbow acting as a fulcrum. This full-arm vibrato is the only sort effective for the double bass. The cellist, of course, can employ the wrist vibrato too, and the violinist, the finger and wrist vibrati. But these instruments do not require the use of so much force to press the string down. The full-arm vibrato of the bass player is a sideways motion, not a rolling one. Once the hand begins to roll, you get into trouble. At that point go back to the table exercise, one hand at a time.

Finally, vibrato is a moving thing; it does not stop when the note stops. If you are playing moving notes, the vibrato must move along with them. But when you come to a sustained note, don't relax in tone. In fact, unless the music directs otherwise, you may want to make a slight crescendo that leads into the next passage, and with it, keep the vibrato going so that the tone level keeps up. Frequently major orchestras will be told by conductors to keep the tone up, just as the individual player must do. Good bass players keep the tone going; the vibrato continues even when changing from one note to another. It is most important to think in large phrases and not to chop up the musical line. While looking outward, look inward—listen to and criticize yourself, for what is important to the individual player becomes magnified for the orchestra as a whole.

III.

Preparing for a Career

No matter how accomplished a bassist you may be, you are never far from teaching, to a greater or lesser degree. If you are a student, you generally assimilate more than you expend. If you are a teacher, you impart your musical knowledge and wisdom to your students more so than when playing in a symphony orchestra, where you implement the ideas of the conductor. It is in the lesson, though, that the student and professional meet. To have or to give a good lesson, it is necessary to understand the dynamics at work.

LESSONS, CLINICS, CLASSES

When a student comes to a teacher for the first time, the teacher should ask him what he plans to do as a bass player. Does he intend to play in a symphony orchestra, or does he intend to teach? In many cases he may want to do both. In the former case, the student should be started on orchestral excerpts, should learn the styles, the ways, and the means of symphony orchestras. This student can take a full dose of the technical aspects of playing. In the case of the student who intends to teach, the emphasis is somewhat different. Here, the teacher should relate the student's playing to his other activities, and should teach pedagogy, especially showing the student how to analyze his own problems. By this method the student will be able to teach others.

Imitative and Analytic Learning

A similar method of assessing the capability of the more advanced student has been used by Janos Starker, world-famous cellist and professor at Indiana University, and Victor Aitay, co-concertmaster of the Chicago Symphony. They assess whether the student has learned his instrument by imitating, following the instructions of others, or whether he has learned it by analyzing his own playing. The imitative player may speak of not knowing what studies to practice, of not having a big enough sound, or of not being able to do this or that. The analytic player, on the other hand, may speak of not being able to control the speed of his bow, correct the positions, or control his wrist. The first student deals in generalities, the second in specifics. One speaks of effects, the other of causes. The teacher will have to decide whether the distinction is the result of temperament or training, and adjust accordingly. Once the diagnosis has been made, the teacher can progress to the treatment. The imitative musician needs to be shown the value of being analytic, and to this end the teacher should stress technique. The analytic player needs to imitate. A balance of the imitative and analytic factors is essential in approaching a piece of music. The advanced player intending to play professionally will generally have a strong imitative musical sense. Hence he should learn to analyze his playing. Conversely, the analytic student, whether pursuing a career or not, should be made to imitate, to think of effects, and to concentrate on the overall musical idea.

Imitative and analytic players need not feel that the problems they encounter are theirs alone. The musical problem a concerto may pose must be recognized, mastered, and expressed in musical terms by all those players who attempt the work. Likewise, a technical problem posed by a piece points up not just one player's limitations, but those of many. In other words, in either situation the problems are rarely unique. If the student has a high intellectual capacity for abstraction, this should be exploited and his analytic powers developed. If he is an instinctive player, it is best to use the analytic technique but to delay disclosing the fact for as long as possible. In this way the teacher's technique and musicianship will not smother those of the student, who must be assisted to develop within himself the capability of criticizing (analyzing) and creating (expressing or imitating in the Aristotelian sense). It is most important that the player become musically and technically self-sufficient.

It is important to make the student aware of, but not cowed by, the technical problems of playing a bass. The student with an inborn musical sense, especially one with good agility, can frequently make an effective showing with a passage by "faking." This kind of playing will be exposed, however, when the student is made to play in slow motion. Such a student needs to concentrate on technique, since he already has enough musical steam to get him through. In contrast, the student who is less musical will frequently concentrate on technique to the detriment of musicality. Here, the musical aspect of playing should be emphasized. Both the technical and musical aspects of a piece can be approached in various ways that can be equally effective in achieving a musical interpretation. Consider the bass solo that begins the slow movement of Mahler's First Symphony:

Feierlich und gemessen, ohne zu schleppen

This passage can be played with or without vibrato, without expression, or with a slight crescendo, depending on the conductor's interpretation. Another example is the recitative from Beethoven's Ninth Symphony, which also yields as many interpretations as there are musicians:

The first two notes can be bowed "up-down," or "down-down," depending on the desired effect. The number of interpretations is unlimited. Whatever the interpretation, it should underline the unusual in contrast to the expected.

Teacher and Student

In the lesson student and teacher work together to get the most from the particular music at hand. The student, to develop his individual interpretation, must relate to the music he is playing by drawing from within himself. As Marshall McLuhan has said, it is necessary to listen with all the senses. The student has the responsibility to approach his lesson as if it were a performance. To this end he should learn his etudes so well that he can play a set of variations on them if called upon to do so. He should understand the music so well that he grasps the principles the composer is putting across, yet be able to develop his own interpretation. In this way the student learns to teach himself. The teacher then acts as a coach, one who offers ideas only when the student has none of his own that are viable.

Sometimes this means trying things that are new. One teacher of many years' experience said that there are no poor students, only poor teachers. The teacher must be quick to initiate new ideas and to invent new ideas to teach. He will not have all the solutions, and he may well raise more problems than he solves. In studying a language the beginning student is told to say words, to pay attention only to their sounds. He memorizes these sounds and learns the patterns of intonation. Later, he is introduced to the meaning of words. The bass student also needs to concentrate on sound.

This bass teacher-coach tries to excite interest in the bass and in music. Rather than talking about the tortures of practicing, he spends time in experimenting with the best expression of musical ideas. The teacher must be flexible and able to relate technical problems to musical ones. Too often teachers slide into the kind of lesson that becomes a checklist of faults in intonation, fingering, and bowing. The student may well be deficient in these respects, but more important, does he have a musical understanding of the piece? Does he hear the sounds? The general musical outline must be sketched definitely before the technical niceties are filled in. That means relating to the student. Teaching music is teaching people. A teacher should take on only as many students as he can have a personal interest in.

What of the person whose talent is limited? Music has traditionally been considered valuable for its ability to develop insight and discipline. For this reason, *musica speculativa* was included in the curriculum of Medieval and Renaissance universities. Even the poor student will benefit as a person from the discipline of mastering just one piece of music well. If he can play just a couple of solos, he should be able to transfer that accomplishment to something that lies better within his talents. Often young students who want to play in a symphony love music enough, but don't have the temperament to make the grade. There are other occupations connected with a symphony, however; orchestras need stage managers, librarians, general managers, personnel managers. There must be someone to see that the symphony gets from place to place, a tour director who knows many languages fluently and can get even suspicious-looking musicians past even more suspicious customs officers.

To return to that student-teacher relationship. There is a good teacher who says very little during his lessons. His students may go for a year or two without knowing if they are any good. One summer one of this teacher's students was tipped off that his teacher really could offer a lot if his brains were picked by asking questions. After a year, the teacher told this student that he was the most interesting one he had ever had. Why? Because the student had made that introverted teacher open up. It is frequently up to the student to ask, to think of questions, to formulate ideas to try on his teacher. The process of learning has to be a working relationship between two musicians trying to solve the same problem. The relationship has to go back and forth as in a game of tennis. If the teacher says, "I'll ask all the questions, and you, student, answer them," the student won't make much musical headway.

It is important that the teacher also be a performer. There is the story about the woodwind class teacher who in the last few years had retired from playing and was teaching bassoon by the book alone. One of his students, a competent bassoonist, offered the information that a suggested fingering was no longer used. The student was thrown out of the class for being impertinent. Changes do occur, of course. Here the teacher could have learned from the student. Education, after all, is about change.

Both partners have their responsibilities. The teacher can lead the way, but the student will have to do the work. The teacher should evaluate the student's performance honestly. He should give an objective criticism, though it may be painful. This is one of the few times that the player can get a true evaluation of his playing.

A music teacher should get to know his professional counterpart. Together they make a good team. Some universities with good music schools and most conservatories have this interaction. The professional can sometimes give the music educator some ideas on the methods of teaching, and vice versa. The one-to-one relationship in the private lesson is necessary, but it should be augmented by master classes, ideally held once a month, when each student plays for perhaps twenty minutes. In this way students can develop a concept of style, and can harden their nerves by playing for each other. And what an incentive for practicing! One bad experience resulting from insufficient practice guarantees that the student will thereafter practice diligently. All excuses are lame when you are onstage before the judgment of your peers, who are often harsher in their criticism than the teacher. At one gathering of bass players from six major universities there was a recital by two performers from each university, the whole event topped off by a performance by Gary Karr. He said that he had never been so nervous before large audiences as he was when he had to play in front of this small group of about seventy-five bass players and teachers. After playing for your colleagues and for others who are strangers, it will seem easier to play for a conductor. Such an experience is excellent training for auditions. The old European practice of having all the students get together in the evening to play something (even if it is just a scale played with a good tone and in tune) helps to stimulate new ideas and build courage.

It is also a good way to find out if you really want to perform. What looks enjoyable from one side of the footlights may be an ordeal from the other side. You may overreact in such a situation. You may really hate it. Some years ago there was a bass player from Wilmington, Delaware, who managed to get into the conservatory, but played rather poorly. His teacher would ask, "How are the cabbages down in Wilmington?" Some years later this student looked back on his conservatory days and realized they were just what he had needed: he found out that cabbages, not basses, were for him. Now he owns three stores, a yacht, and a summer home. You need a strong streak of the extrovert to enjoy performing music. You must enjoy theatrical success and want to try for it again.

A good testing place for ideas and performance are the many music camps and festivals that are held throughout the country each summer. Here the young musician can rub elbows with the famous and can get a feel for the profession. Bass players come from all over to play, listen, and to criticize each other. This experience firms up the nerves for performance but, more importantly, it introduces new ideas and develops flexibility in interpretation and technique.

The interaction we have been talking about has one very important effect. It is not only a test of the student but of the teacher as well. If the teacher's theories are wrong, the students are never going to get better. If his students do not measure up to those of other teachers, he should take stock of what he is doing and change his ways.

The bass player should listen to others of his breed. There are the recordings of great bass players: Bertram Turetzky and Gary Karr today, Serge Koussevitsky in the mid-twenties, and others less known. Get to know what bass play-

ers are doing in other parts of the world, for their approach may be quite different from yours. The bassist especially needs to see others of his kind to keep from feeling like a musical outcast, and to allow him to measure himself against his colleagues. The bass, like its player, is a sociable instrument.

The bass is no longer the ugly duckling of the orchestra, alone and awkward. It is more and more becoming a first-class instrument, partly because of better instruments and strings, but principally because of better players. As recently as forty years ago the bass was considered by many to be a musical joke. Then, it was a challenge to do anything with it or with its critics. Today, bassists have met that challenge.

ORCHESTRAL PLAYING

Orchestral playing takes a good knowledge of the orchestral and operatic literature and an understanding of ensemble playing. The bass part may not always be important, but the bass has the advantage of being able to survey the entire orchestra as the conductor does. The conductor and violist Vladimir Bakaleinikoff said: "The best conductors are bass players or percussion players." Koussevitsky was a bassist, Fritz Reiner a percussionist. The less expressive instruments, or at least those with limited repertoire, often provide the best conductors. Like Bakaleinikoff, Pierre Monteux was a violist. Toscanini was a cellist. Ormandy, a violinist, is the exception. These musicians have had to make up for a less gratifying part as instrumentalists by developing the ability to listen to the totality of the music.

Passages

As the student progresses in his studies, and even as early as the first position, it is a good idea to introduce orchestral passages. There is nothing quite like using the real thing in your studies. You don't make it to the top in the musical world as an interpreter of Franz Simandl's *Gradus ad Parnassum*. Orchestral excerpts help expand the breadth of the bassist. If the passages are taught according to the styles of the various orchestras, they take on further meaning. Most traditional bass method books do not use contemporary examples. These too should be learned, since they will most certainly appear in the programs of symphony orchestras. One bass teacher, when asked by one of his students about learning orchestral excerpts said: "There's a room over there where you can learn them if you wish." This attitude is a mistake. The bass is a gregarious instrument. Not long ago a conductor of one of our major symphony orchestras, after listening to a dozen candidates for principal bass, threw up his hands and said, "Throw these canaries out! I want to hear a double bass!" After twenty years of playing, John Schafer, principal bass of the New York Philharmonic Orchestra, said he still got a thrill out of orchestral music. With him at the time was Yashi Barowski, the first violinist of the Curtis String Quartet, who just chuckled and said "I look at the Philadelphia Orchestra . . . the first violins are all miserable because they're not concert artists, the seconds are miserable because they're not first violinists, and the violas are miserable because they had to give up the violin. The only happy ones in the string section are the bass players, because when they took up the bass they knew that they were going to be orchestral players." The only possible exceptions are Dragonetti and Bottesini, and we do not really know how they felt or fared, what they wanted out of life besides playing the bass. There just isn't much room for a solo bassist. Even today there are very few. After hearing a very good bass soloist, a famous concert cellist said, "It's phenomenal, but I don't know if I would want to hear it a second time." It is difficult enough for the violinist to become a concert artist, and cellists have even more problems. If the bass player is serious about playing, that means playing in an orchestra. This must be the outlet for the bass player's musicality. To this end, he should divide his practice time in thirds: one third on scales, arpeggios, exercises, and tone production; a third on solos; and no less than a third on orchestral parts. Often the good bassist may feel a certain frustration because of the limited repertoire and limited role for him in the orchestra. He can take some Baroque music written for the pleasure of all instruments and transcribe it for the bass. The Bach gamba suites and, of course, the cello suites are excellent material for this.

Bass players are creative or they wouldn't be musicians. To some degree that creativity must be controlled, though, since orchestral musicians must yield their wills to that of the conductor. Some players discover that teaching can be creative. Certainly, creating players is a viable and useful outlet. The bassist rarely plays in chamber music, with the notable exception of the Schubert "Trout" Quintet. He's called on to play that so often that he practically knows it by heart. He can learn another instrument in order to play chamber music—and some have taken this extreme measure. One side benefit from this is that his orchestral bass playing should improve, since he will now be inclined to listen to other voices in the orchestra. There is the old story about the father and son who played together in the opera orchestra. Finally the great day came when one of them could arise out of the pit and take the night off. The father gave the son the chance. The son decided to go out into the audience and watch the opera that night, *Carmen*. At intermission the son rushed backstage, telling his father, "You know that melody that we have in the last act that goes:

Well, there's another one going on above us that goes this way":

Ensemble

The bass player should see orchestral playing from the standpoint of the music as a whole. He and the conductor have the vantage to do this. Admitted, some parts are a bore. It *is* frustrating that the bass is often subordinated. And the conductor may ask for something that grates against the musical soul. But you do it cheerfully. Your section leader may call for a bowing that fits him but not you. Again you do it his way cheerfully. Orchestral playing is ensemble playing. If you listen and watch, using your other senses (what is the fragrance of a quarter note?), you will be a better musician. This is what a conductor appreciates. He looks at the score and sees things coming. The bass part must fit into a sequence of entrances, and if the bassist can see the pattern, he will be able to do a better job with his part. As in the other arts, especially drama and ballet, timing is important. In ballet, when a ballerina leaps into the air, she expects to be caught. Likewise, catch your bass entrance at precisely the right moment.

AUDITIONS

Auditions require a demonstrable musical capacity and facility with the instrument, knowledge of the orchestral literature, and the ability to keep going. Add to these the knack for intuiting conductors.

Solos

Come prepared for your audition with a Baroque sonata, a contemporary piece, something fast, something slow—pieces that show off your mastery of the instrument. Some players have been hired only on their ability to play solos. These solos are your calling card. These pieces must be played well. You are competing at times with candidates whose sole study has been solos. It is probably a good idea these days not to play the Eccles Sonata, since conductors have heard it from bass players so often. This is a pity, since the first movement is probably the most musical piece in the bass repertoire. Try one of the Bach gamba sonatas, the Koussevitsky Concerto, the Bottesini Introduction and Allegro, the Hindemith Sonata—something that lies well for you. Your solo should show off your musicianship and technique as quickly as possible. To these ends, choose a slow and a fast movement that together total no more than about four minutes. Some orchestras, like the Chicago Symphony, allow less than fifteen minutes for auditions. If the solo is too long, the conductor rightly begins to fidget; four minutes is ample time for him to realize your worth. The important thing is for the solo to show your mastery of the range of the instrument as succinctly as possible so that you can then demonstrate your sensitivity and adaptability in playing orchestral passages.

Conductors

Know the idiosyncrasies of different conductors. For instance, Reiner called for a little Viennese hesitation in the pickup to the Scherzo of the Beethoven Fifth Symphony, whereas Frenchman Jean Martinon said definitely not—no pause between the pick up and the first note of the next measure, and the other times that that figure occurs:

(2nd time *p*)

Exploit the richness of the passage and avoid the 1 2 3, 1 2 3 interpretation that is all too common. Generally there are several ways to make musical sense out of a passage. For example, in the fugal section from the last movement of Mozart's G Minor Symphony you can play the first two notes in each entrance marcato or legato:

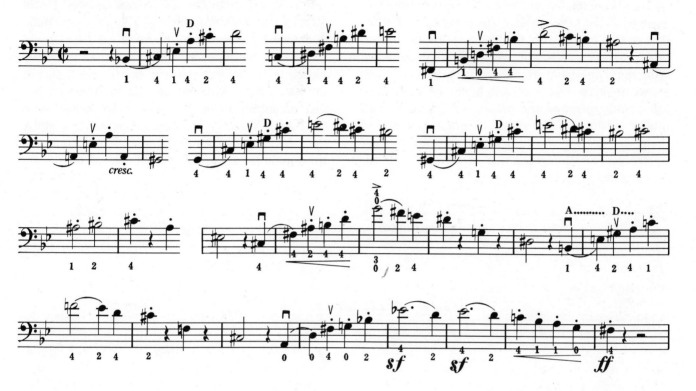

Before playing an audition for an orchestra, understand that orchestra's individuality. What makes it sound the way it does? What gives it its particular character? Eugene Ormandy sometimes has his assistant conductor vary the tempos in auditions to see if the candidate can follow the beat. In such cases don't lecture the conductor or show him how it should go, just smile and do as he says. This is probably one of the most important things the conductor is looking for— the talent for following the stick. Watch the conductor as he sets the tempo in his own mind; his head, hand, or foot will probably establish the tempo, and by observing him closely, you will be able to anticipate the tempo he wants, leaving you free to concentrate from the start upon nuances of interpretation. Play boldly, freely, in an operatic sytle, and emphasize tone. But as you stretch certain passages, be sure not to distort the tempo beyond what the conductor wants. Reach a balance between the slow, stretching tempo that shows off your musical soul and the faster one in the context of the piece that the conductor may often indicate.

Now, the matter of playing the notes. Try to play all the notes in the difficult passages, but it is impossible to have all of Strauss, Mozart, and Beethoven under your fingers all the time. If you're in an audition and suddenly find something on the stand that you haven't seen for two years, remember the finger patterns, and chances are your fingers will respond. They have a long memory. Leave it to them to get you through. Use your muscle memory and your ear, and never mind about reading. At least know the tune and the finger patterns. If you know the fingering and can sing the passage, you'll probably be able to play it. If you find that you can't get through all the notes, make a joyful noise and just keep the tempo going. Musicality above all. If you have played several of the things well and demonstrated that you do know over half of what you were asked to play, and if you happen to get stuck on one passage, at least follow the conductor and keep playing. He knows that when a piece is programmed the musicians have at least a week before the first rehearsal to look at it. If you have good facility, you will be able to review the passage. The conductor in an audition is primarily interested to see if you watch his baton.

Repertoire

Find out what music your prospective orchestra is playing the next season or that next week. Get recordings of the music, particularly if you are auditioning for an opera orchestra, where so many of the conventions are unwritten. Follow the music along with the score, marking particular passages. When it comes time to audition, you may not have as much experience as some other players, but you will have the advantage of having reviewed the music. In listening to as many versions of the music as possible you may help yourself win the audition by showing a richer interpretation. Interpretation sometimes calls for more than musical sensitivity. In operas, oratorios, and some symphonies it can be important to understand the dramatic content of what you are playing. For example, you can make better sense of the solo for the basses in Act IV of Verdi's opera *Otello* when you know that Otello is entering Desdemona's bedroom to kill her and then kill himself; he enters, as Shakespeare phrases it, to "put out the light, and then put out the light." Remember that Desdemona has just made her peace with the world in her prayer, "Ave Maria." Her aria ends on a high A flat. In complete contrast, the next entrance is the double basses' low E, played pianissimo:

As Otello enters, this rising motif is repeated three times in variant form, just as the Moor kisses his wife three times. He asks her to confess her supposed adultery, and when she again claims she is innocent, he strangles her. Otello's quick ferocity is suggested in the passage that ends the solo:

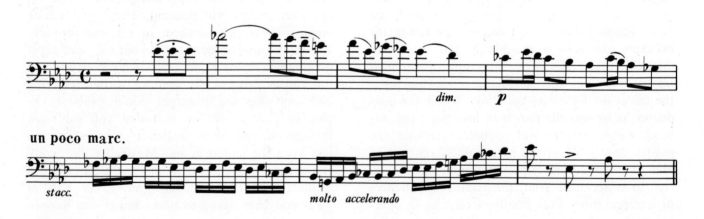

Obviously, it helps to know the story.

Likewise, in *Rigoletto* the duet for bass and cello that serves as a prelude to Act II should be regarded in its context. The duet begins:

34

Marullo and others have abducted Rigoletto's daughter Gilda, and ironically the Duke learns this from a chorus that suggests, in its use of half steps, other intervals, and rhythm, the earlier instrumental duet:

Scor – ren – do u – ni ·ti remo – ta vi – a

When Rigoletto enters, disconsolate at his daughter's fate, he must for politic reasons appear to be jocose. Again, the motif, now in minor, recalls the duet in rhythm and intervals. This time it is almost inverted; certainly here it is used in a perverted sense:

La rà, la rà, la rà, la rà, la rà, la rà, la rà,

It is especially important in operas to know the situation on stage, but it is sometimes just as important to understand the textual meaning in symphonies. To render well the recitative in Beethoven's Ninth Symphony it helps to recognize that the double basses herald the baritone's solo that appears some 124 bars later. The words of the singer, "O Freude, nicht diese Töne," then "sondern lasst uns angenehmere anstimmen," and finally: "und freudenvollere" ("O friends, not these sounds, but let us begin to sing agreeable ones, and be full of joy"), should help to interpret Beethoven's musical meaning in the earlier instrumental passage. One caution, however. Do not be carried away by the dramatics of the moment. The underlying 3/4 meter must be present. Use the text to ascertain the architecture of the passage and to know where to breathe, to change bows. As always, learn to sing such passages before playing them, particularly if there are words too. Know the context in which you are playing. That too is musicianship.

It helps to know what other passages you may be asked to play. For years conductors pulled out Strauss' *Til Eulenspiegel* and *Don Juan*. But the bass players got wise, and now that they know these, the conductors have turned to the more difficult *Ein Heldenleben* and *Also Sprach Zarathustra*. If you can play these four and *Don Quixote*, Strauss should be no problem. The Mozart symphonies that are most often used in auditions are, in order of frequency, numbers 40, 35, 41, 39, 38, 37. The particular passages from these symphonies can be found in excerpt books, or you can ask your bass teacher which they are. These Mozart symphonies each have three main themes—some very energetic, others lyrical. It is important in studying them that you make each one different so that your interpretation makes use of contrast. The Beethoven symphonies in order of most frequent use are numbers 5, 9, then 7, 3, 8, 1, 6, and 4. With Beethoven it is best to know all the symphonies well. Once in a while you get something unusual, such as Berlioz's *Symphonie Fantastique,* or one of the symphonies or piano concertos by Rachmaninoff. From the works of Brahms, conductors like to pick out the slow movements to see if you can sustain passages.

Certain other orchestral passages are frequently asked for: the Ginastera Variations, the Prokofiev *Lieutenant Kije Suite,* and the Mahler First Symphony. In this last, most conductors want the bass solo of the slow movement played without expression and vibrato. Find out what your conductor wants. As a suggestion, when playing the Mahler, tune the G string up to A. Know also the Mendelssohn *Scottish* and *Italian* symphonies. Oscar Zimmerman's editions of the complete orchestral parts are better to study than the excerpts, since through them you can develop the timing that comes from having the entire part. Study the score too. The conductor Victor Alessandro once said: "Count the beats in between, because we know the score and we are hearing everything else that is going on in the orchestra." If you skip a beat, the conductor will think you do not understand the music. The conductor hears the whole piece, and he doesn't want a bass player who plays his part and hears nothing else.

You should know certain orchestral passages from memory. These are the recitative from Beethoven's Ninth Symphony, the Scherzo from the Fifth, and the long passage from the first movement of the Seventh.

Opera passages are also used by conductors for auditions, expecially in Europe. Your ability to play on the lower strings is tested in *Otello*, and your lyric capacity by *Rigoletto*. These are musts. Conductors further expect you to know Wagner (*Der Fliegende Holländer, Die Walküre,* and *Die Meistersinger*), and the standard Verdi and Rossini operas.

Finally, besides repertoire there are other things to know about playing auditions. No matter what you're playing, watch and follow the conductor's beat. He also wants to see if you can play lyrically, if you can control your bow, and if you are a musician as well as a technician. Auditions, then, are a matter of communicating by means of musical dialogue with the conductor.

Tactics

Other non-musical factors bear on auditions. Most often we practice in a small room. Then when the day comes for the audition we find we are swallowed in the darkness of a large concert hall. Try to practice in the hall itself, if possible. The sound, you will find, is very different. Practicing in a small room inhibits your dynamic range and makes your playing too refined, at least too refined for the concert hall. Like a large painting, your playing must be conceived and related to the expanse of the hall. In this way the crudities do not show, just as the brush strokes blend together in a painting viewed at a distance. Match the fineness of your playing to the location.

Some conductors conduct auditions, not in a formal fashion, but in a way designed to put the bassist at ease. The maestro will excuse himself for one reason or another (to check on box office receipts, to pay the milkman, or consult with the fourth horn on getting the pedal point), but during that time when he asks you to play a few scales to warm up, he may be giving you your audition. Play those scales, those arpeggios, that etude, and that solo, not simply as warm-up material, which it may well be, but play them as if your life or livelihood depended upon them, for it may. Make every note count.

Familiarity with things at audition time helps calm you. If you have a good instrument, take it with you to your audition; don't bet on a dark horse, it may have a C neck. Go to the city where the audition is to be held at least a day early. Find a place to stay, to eat, and check out the concert hall. No photo finishes where you race up to the front of the hall, toss the keys to the doorman, grab the bass and waddle quickly inside. Besides playing poorly, the audition produces ulcers. Enjoy your audition—at least you know your audience is listening to you, so make the most of such an opportunity.

Playing the double bass well is much more than pumping out downbeats to Strauss waltzes and Verdi arias, though the bass is certainly effective here. It calls for technical skill, but more important, an intimate knowledge of the music and a sensitive rapport with the ensemble. The bass *is* a musical instrument.

11 12 ● 80 79 78 77 76 75 74 73